Boredom Busters

Create Crazy Crafts, Mad Models and Funny Faces
with Post-it® Notes

Debbie MacKinnon

Hi! I'm Pete!

and I'm Patch!

A Fireside Book
Published by Simon & Schuster
New York London Toronto Sydney

We'll help you make lots of cool projects with Post-it® Notes. Just follow our simple instructions for a Boredom Busting time!

FIRESIDE
Rockefeller Center
1230 Avenue of the Americas
New York, NY 10020

For information regarding special discounts for bulk
purchases, please contact Simon & Schuster Special Sales
at 1-800-456-6798 or business@simonandschuster.com

Manufactured in China

10 9 8 7 6 5 4 3 2 1

Library of Congress Cataloging-in-Publication Data
MacKinnon, Debbie.
    Post-it®: Boredom busters: create crazy crafts,
    mad models and funny faces with Post-it® Notes/
    Debbie MacKinnon.
        p. cm.
    "A Fireside book."
    1. Paper work—Juvenile literature.
    2. Sticky notes—Juvenile literature. I. Title.
    TT870. M15 2005
    745.54—dc22   2005048959

ISBN-13: 978-0-7432-8432-5
ISBN-10:   0-7432-8432-1

Conceived and produced by Weldon Owen Pty Ltd
59 Victoria Street, McMahons Point
Sydney, NSW 2060, Australia

CHIEF EXECUTIVE OFFICER John Owen
PRESIDENT Terry Newell
PUBLISHER Sheena Coupe
CREATIVE DIRECTOR Sue Burk
PRODUCTION MANAGER Louise Mitchell
PRODUCTION COORDINATOR Monique Layt
VICE PRESIDENT INTERNATIONAL SALES Stuart Laurence
ADMINISTRATOR INTERNATIONAL SALES Kristine Ravn

DESIGNER Sue Rawkins
DESIGN ASSISTANT Juliana Titin
PHOTOGRAPHY Stuart Bowey/Adlibitum
ILLUSTRATIONS Lionel Portier, Sue Rawkins
EDITORIAL ASSISTANT Jessica Cox
EDITORIAL COORDINATOR Helen Flint

Color reproduction by Colourscan Overseas Co Pte Ltd
Printed by SNP LeeFung Printers

A Weldon Owen Production

Pete says:
I hope you'll enjoy
creating all these cool
projects with us!

Contents

What you'll need

■ Have lots of fun making cool stuff with Post-it® Notes on even the rainiest days! You'll need a few extra bits and pieces, along with your notes, to make all the Boredom Busters projects. You probably have most of these things at home anyway.

We have given you lots of Post-it® Notes with this book to help you make great projects, but you'll need some of these tiny ones, too.

Pens and paper

You can add Post-it® Notes to colored paper, cardboard and plain brown bags to make some of our projects. Add decorations and details with your crayons or with felt-tip pens.

Bits and pieces

We used a ping pong ball, colored threads, pipe cleaners, push pins (mind your fingers!) and colored popsicle sticks to make our projects.

Stickers and plates

Make funny faces and crazy decorations on some of the Post-it® Notes with circle- and star-shaped stickers. Keep some paper or plastic plates from a party or picnic to make creative projects with notes.

Post-it® Notes

■ These are the actual sizes of the Post-it® Notes we used to make everything in this book. We have put a little picture, set out like the one shown below, next to each project. This tells you how many notes you will need.

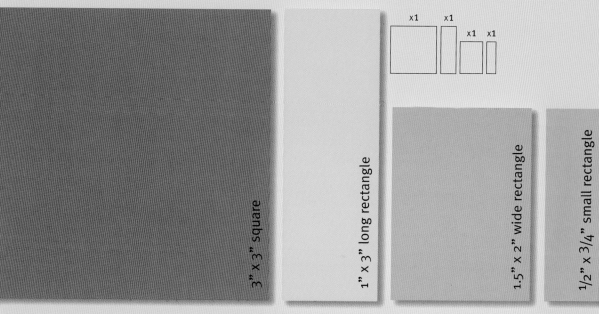

x1 x1 x1 x1

3" x 3" square

1" x 3" long rectangle

1.5" x 2" wide rectangle

1/2" x 3/4" small rectangle

Pete

■ Here's how to make our friendly character, Pete. He will help you create lots of fun things with Post-it® Notes.

Use the Post-it® Notes shown below to make Pete. Set them out on the table in the same way as they are in the picture.

Make Pete's arms, feet and hat by folding some of the notes. Make sure the adhesive strip is in the same place as marked in the picture.

Draw a happy face on Pete.

Hi! My name is Pete!

hat

front view

adhesive strip

Stick Pete's blue T-shirt onto his purple body.

You could write some notes or helpful tips on Pete's T-shirt.

x2   x1   x1   x7

Patch

■ Patch the dog and Pete will help you make your projects.

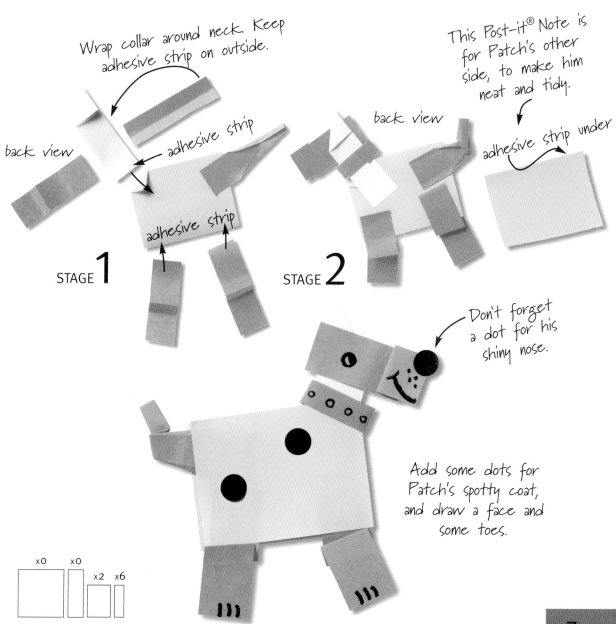

Wrap collar around neck. Keep adhesive strip on outside.

back view

adhesive strip

adhesive strip

STAGE 1

back view

This Post-it® Note is for Patch's other side, to make him neat and tidy.

adhesive strip under

STAGE 2

Don't forget a dot for his shiny nose.

Add some dots for Patch's spotty coat, and draw a face and some toes.

x0   x0   x2   x6

7

S-s-s-snake

■ This slippery snake will slide, slither and hiss at your friends!

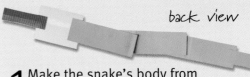

back view

1 Make the snake's body from Post-it® Notes as shown in the picture.

back view

Turn the snake over and add some dots for its eyes and the patterns on its skin.

2 Fold in the edges to make the snake's shape.

| x0 | x3 | x1 | x2 |

Scary spider

■ Make this scary spider and hang it from a string, so you can wiggle and jiggle it.

Make a hole for the thread by pushing the point of a pencil through the Post-it® Note.

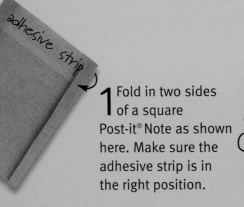

adhesive strip

1 Fold in two sides of a square Post-it® Note as shown here. Make sure the adhesive strip is in the right position.

2 Fold in the edges to make the spider's body. Thread a piece of string or cotton through the hole and knot it securely.

adhesive strip under

adhesive strip

3 Add Post-it® Notes for legs and fold them as shown.

Add some dots for eyes and use a felt-tip pen to draw on the spider's mouth.

4 Add more legs (spiders have eight!) then fold and add the head.

Pete says: Make lots of spiders for a Halloween party!

x1	x0	x1	x8

9

Meet the RoBotties

■ Create a family of RoBotties. The pictures will give you some ideas, but use your imagination to make many more.

Wobbly has dots for eyes.

Wobbly RoBottie

back view

Stick stars onto Wobbly's body and add his name.

WOBBLY

To make the wobbly arms, legs and necks, fold long Post-it® Notes into zigzags.

x1   x7   x1   x6

Big RoBottie

Pink
RoBottie

Spottie RoBottie

Pete says:
Use all kinds of
dots and stars to
decorate your
RoBotties!

Tiny RoBottie

11

Elephant and giraffe

Add a dot for the elephant's eye and draw on his tusk.

Put on a glove and your fingers become the legs.

■ Make this elephant and giraffe, then put on a glove and use your fingers for their legs. You'll have lots of fun with these great puppets!

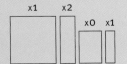

x1 x2 x0 x1

1 Fold a square Post-it® Note as shown to the right. Then fold a long note in half for the trunk. Fold the bottom corner.

2 Tuck the trunk into the body and stick a long strip behind for the ear. Fold as shown. Use a small folded note for the elephant's tail.

adhesive strip

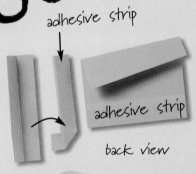

adhesive strip

back view

adhesive strip

front view

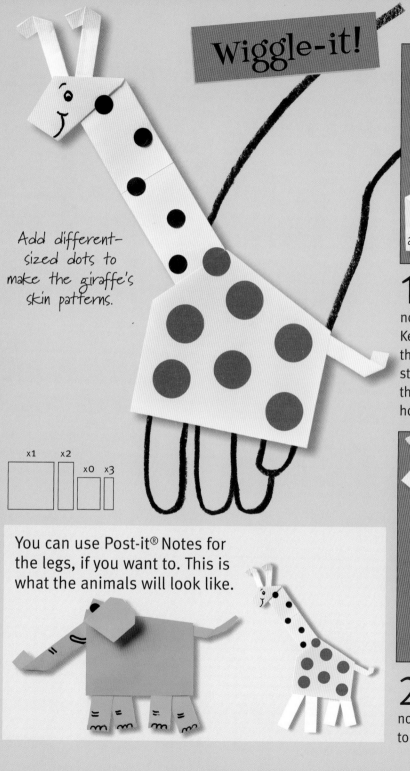

Wiggle-it!

Add different-sized dots to make the giraffe's skin patterns.

x1 x2 x0 x3

You can use Post-it® Notes for the legs, if you want to. This is what the animals will look like.

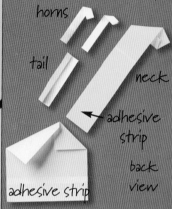

horns

tail

neck

adhesive strip

adhesive strip

back view

1 Fold a square Post-it® Note for the body. Join two long notes to make the neck. Keep the adhesive strip at the bottom of the neck to stick onto the body. Fold three small notes for the horns and tail.

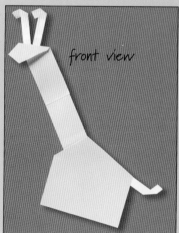

front view

2 This is the front view. You can see how the notes stick together to make the giraffe.

13

Making a square

■ Make a Post-it® Note square so you can fold fun origami projects. We have shown the square actual size to help you follow our simple steps.

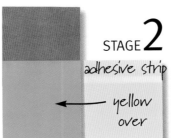

STAGE 2

adhesive strip

← yellow over

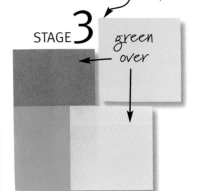

adhesive strip under

STAGE 3 green over

STAGE 1

adhesive strip

blue over | adhesive strip

Join four square Post-it® Notes together as shown in the pictures. Keep the edges straight. To make the square strong, you must have the adhesive strips in the right places.

Make your square on top of ours to keep the edges straight.

back view

14

Windmill

■ Making a whirling windmill is easy when you follow these simple step-by-step instructions.

front view

1 Make a Post-it® Note square by following the instructions on the opposite page. Fold the sides of the square to the center.

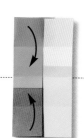

2 Fold the top and bottom of the square into the center.

It will look like this.

3 Reach underneath and pull out the corners of the square into the shape shown.

4 Pull out the bottom half of the windmill in the same way. Fold the top left corner up and the bottom right corner down.

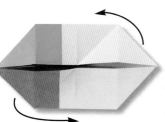

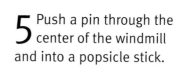

5 Push a pin through the center of the windmill and into a popsicle stick.

Pete says:
Be careful not to stick your finger with the pin.

Fortune teller

■ Once you have learned to make a Post-it® Note square, you can make all kinds of origami projects. Here's how to make a fortune teller. Use it to dazzle your friends.

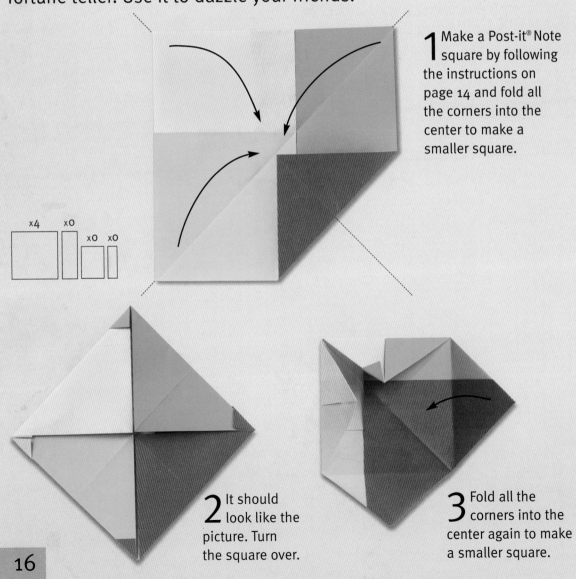

1 Make a Post-it® Note square by following the instructions on page 14 and fold all the corners into the center to make a smaller square.

x4   x0   x0   x0

2 It should look like the picture. Turn the square over.

3 Fold all the corners into the center again to make a smaller square.

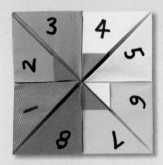

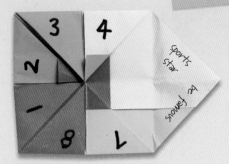

4 Write numbers on the triangles as shown here.

5 Write a message under each number as shown here.

6 Fold the square in half, then in half again.

Put your fingers in here.

1-2-3-4-5

p-i-n-k

Pete says:
Here are some fortune ideas!

- be famous
- go to the moon
- be rich
- meet a movie star
- go to top of the class
- be the most popular
- become a sports star
- win a prize

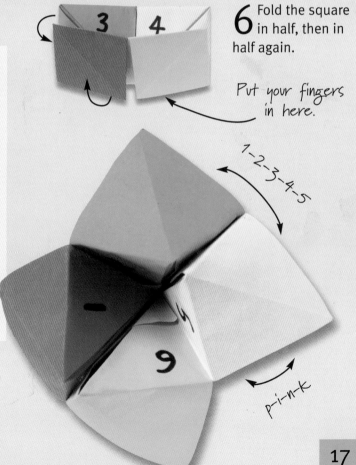

Fly a plane

■ Making a plane is easy with a Post-it® Note square. Instructions are on page 14. Try different models, too.

1 Fold your Post-it® Note square in half.

2 Fold the top corners into the center as shown in the picture.

You could add some stickers on the wings to decorate your plane.

3 Fold the sides into the center again.

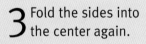

x4   x0   x1   x0

Pete says: Have your own Air Show! Invite your friends over and see whose plane flies the farthest.

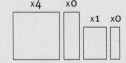

back view

4 Fold the plane in half.

5 Fold back the wings on each side.

6 Turn the plane over and add an extra note to make it more stable.

Chinese dragon

Stars make great eyes and tongue.

Add some colored dots to decorate its tail.

x5   x2   x1   x0

■ Create this fun Chinese dragon, then make it wiggle and stretch.

1 Make a long zigzag shape by folding and joining four square Post-it® Notes.

adhesive strip on outside

back view

2 Add another square note to make the head. Fold it in half with the adhesive strip on the outside. Attach it to the body as shown in the picture.

3 Stick popsicle sticks to the adhesive strips to make the dragon's legs. Use long notes to make its tail.

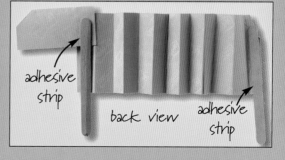

adhesive strip

back view

adhesive strip

Create a crazy cat

■ Make this crazy cat with a paper or plastic plate and lots of different colored Post-it® Notes.

back of plate

x1   x1   x3   x6

Draw the eyes, nose and mouth with a felt-tip pen— then add some dots to finish off the crazy cat.

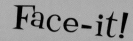

Face-it!

A kooky clown

Make wobbly eyes with
Post-it® Notes folded into
zigzags, topped with
colored dots.

A poochy plate

Pete says:
Use different colored
plates and Post-it® Notes
to make your own
plate creatures.

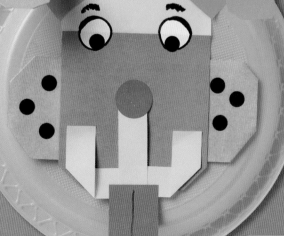

Silly sculpture

■ Have lots of fun building your own free-form sculptures from Post-it® Notes of all shapes and sizes.

1 Join long Post-it® Notes and fold like the ones in the picture. Attach the ends with the adhesive strips to make your shapes. The circle and triangle need three notes each, and the square needs four.

2 Now make lots more shapes and balance one on top of another. Join them all together with long zigzag notes. You can make as many shapes as you like!

Little one slots inside big one.

Super bowling

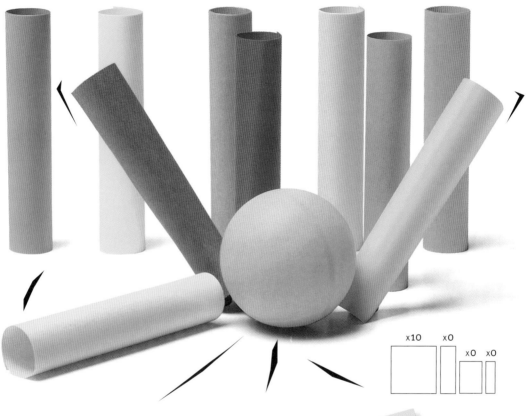

■ Make your own bowling lane with Post-it® Notes rolled into bowling pins. Send a small plastic ball down the lane, and try to knock over as many pins as possible.

adhesive strip

Make a bowling pin by wrapping a note around a pen or pencil.

23

Decorate your door

■ Make a fun sign for your bedroom door. Create a picture on a big sheet of cardboard. Add as many Post-it® Notes as it takes to spell out your name. Use colored dots and stars to decorate your door sign. These ideas will get you started.

A square robot

Add the number of letters in your name.

x1   x2
          x1+?   x3

A puffing train

A creeping caterpillar

Fish mobile

■ Make a fish mobile to hang in your room. It will spin around in the breeze.

back view

Fold to make tail.

1 Stick Post-it® Notes onto a pipe cleaner as shown here. Put another note on top of each one. Keep the adhesive strips at opposite ends so that your fish will stick together.

Add a sticker for its eye and draw on some fish lips.

Use pipe cleaners to hang up your fish.

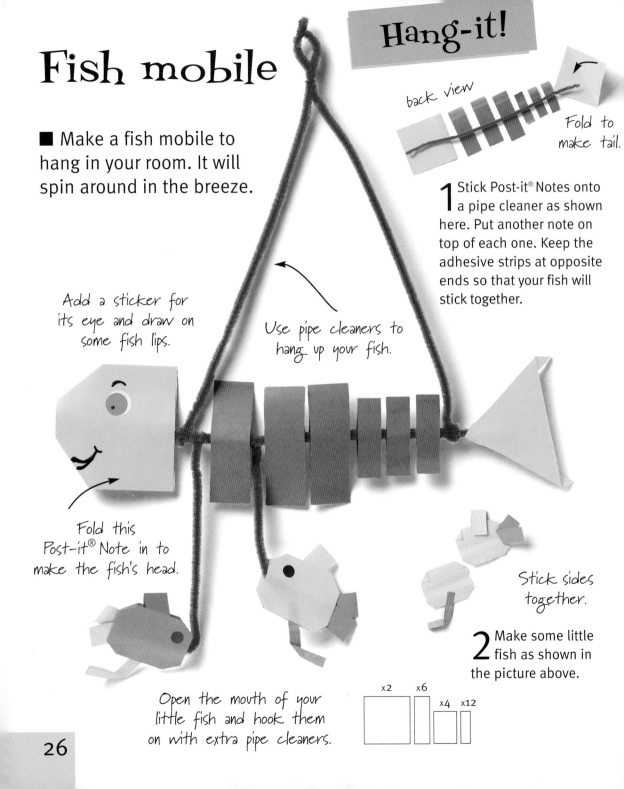

Fold this Post-it® Note in to make the fish's head.

Stick sides together.

2 Make some little fish as shown in the picture above.

Open the mouth of your little fish and hook them on with extra pipe cleaners.

x2   x6   x4   x12

Fish mural

■ Make a monster mural for your wall. Here we have made a floating fish, using mostly square Post-it® Notes. But you can make whatever you like. Change your mural by adding or taking away notes. If you don't have a plain wall, make the mural on a big sheet of paper or cardboard.

Use smaller Post-it® Notes to make the scales, fins and tail.

Pete says:
The more Post-it® Notes you have, the bigger your mural can be!

27

Book-it!

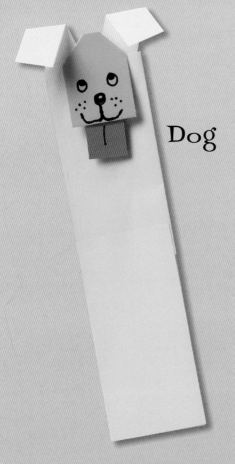

Dog

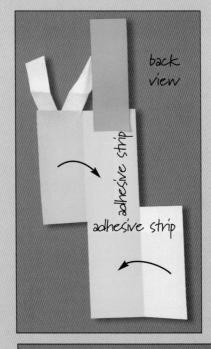

adhesive strip

adhesive strip

1 Fold two square Post-it® Notes and stick them together as shown in the picture. Then add other notes to make the dog's ears and head.

Bookmarks

■ Making bookmarks with Post-it® Notes is easy when you follow these simple steps.

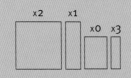

x2   x1
          x0   x3

28

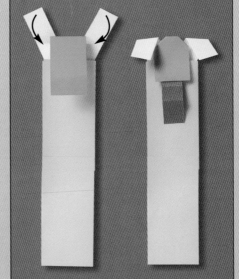

front view

2 Fold down the ears to the front of the bookmark. Shape the dog's head by folding back the top two corners. Stick your dog's tongue behind its head.

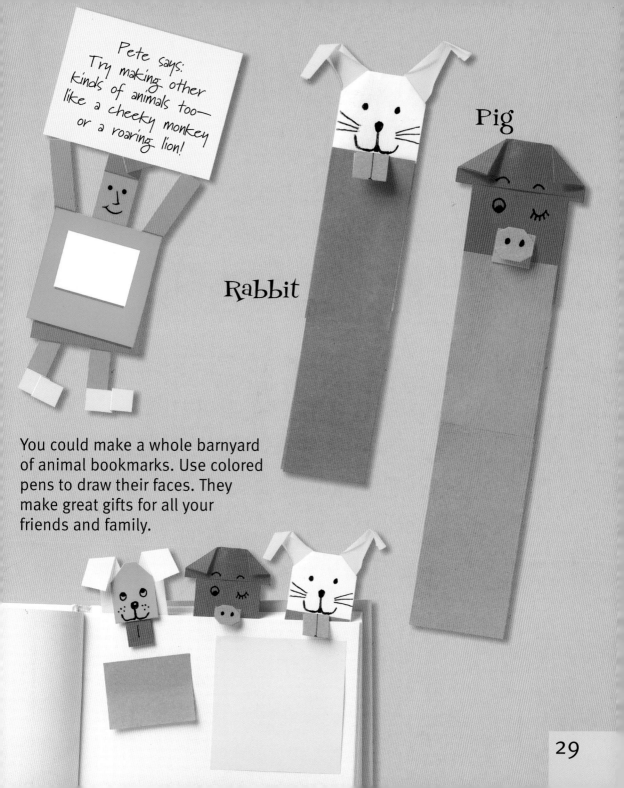

Pete says:
Try making other
kinds of animals too—
like a cheeky monkey
or a roaring lion!

Pig

Rabbit

You could make a whole barnyard
of animal bookmarks. Use colored
pens to draw their faces. They
make great gifts for all your
friends and family.

Brown bag puppets

■ Make a puppet from a brown paper grocery bag. Add as many Post-it® Notes as you like to create some strange and wonderful creatures. Put on a puppet play with your friends.

Lenny the lion

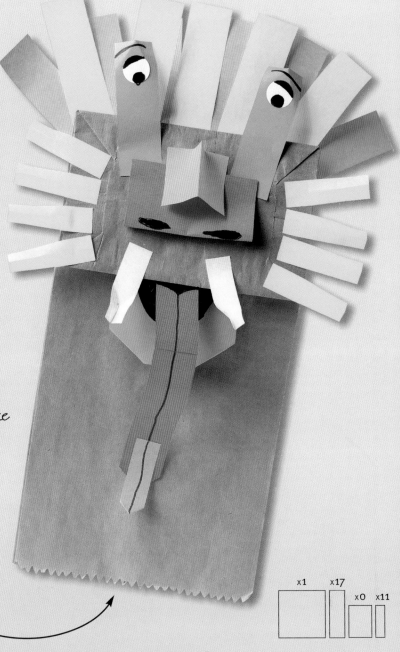

Stick long Post-it® Notes together to make the tongue.

Put your hand inside the bag and wiggle your fingers to make your puppet move.

x1   x17   x0   x11

Perform-it!

Oscar

Make wobbly eyes by folding long Post-it® Notes into zigzags. Then add colored dots.

Toofy

Pete says:
Use lots of dots and stars to make more puppets!

31

Just jewels

Twist the pipe cleaners together to fit your neck or wrist.

■ Wear this fun, colorful jewelry, or make some as presents for your friends.

Necklace and bracelet

Roll small Post-it® Notes around pipe cleaners to make paper beads.

Ring

1 Fold a long Post-it® Note in half. Then roll it up and tuck in the ends as shown to the right.

adhesive strip

2 Decorate your ring with other small Post-it® Notes and stars.

32